Published by

Seedlings

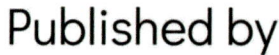

www.kcolemanbooks.com

Want to sing along? Scan this QR code!

SCAN ME

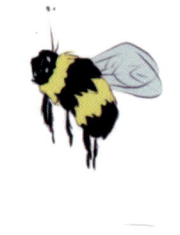

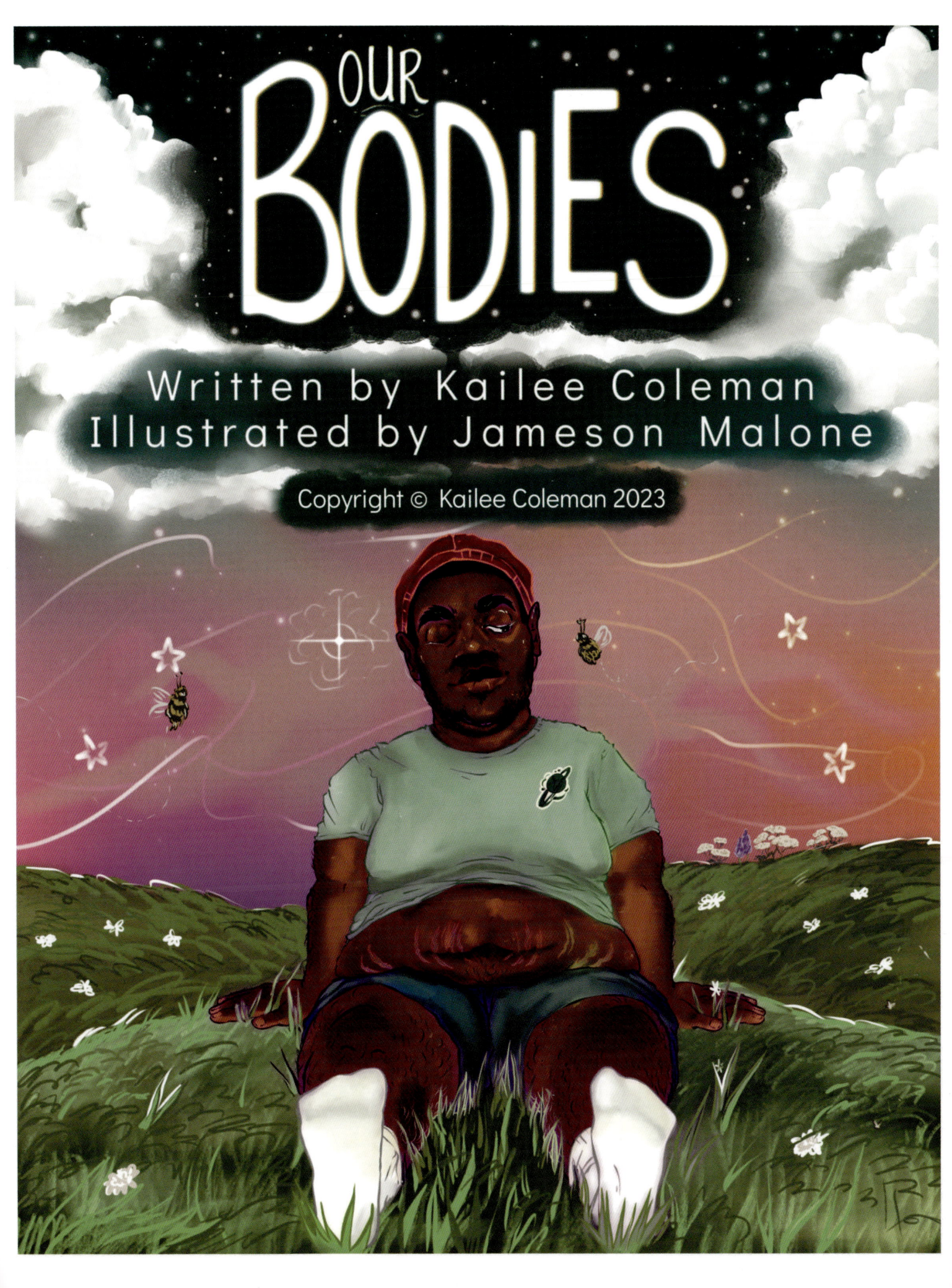

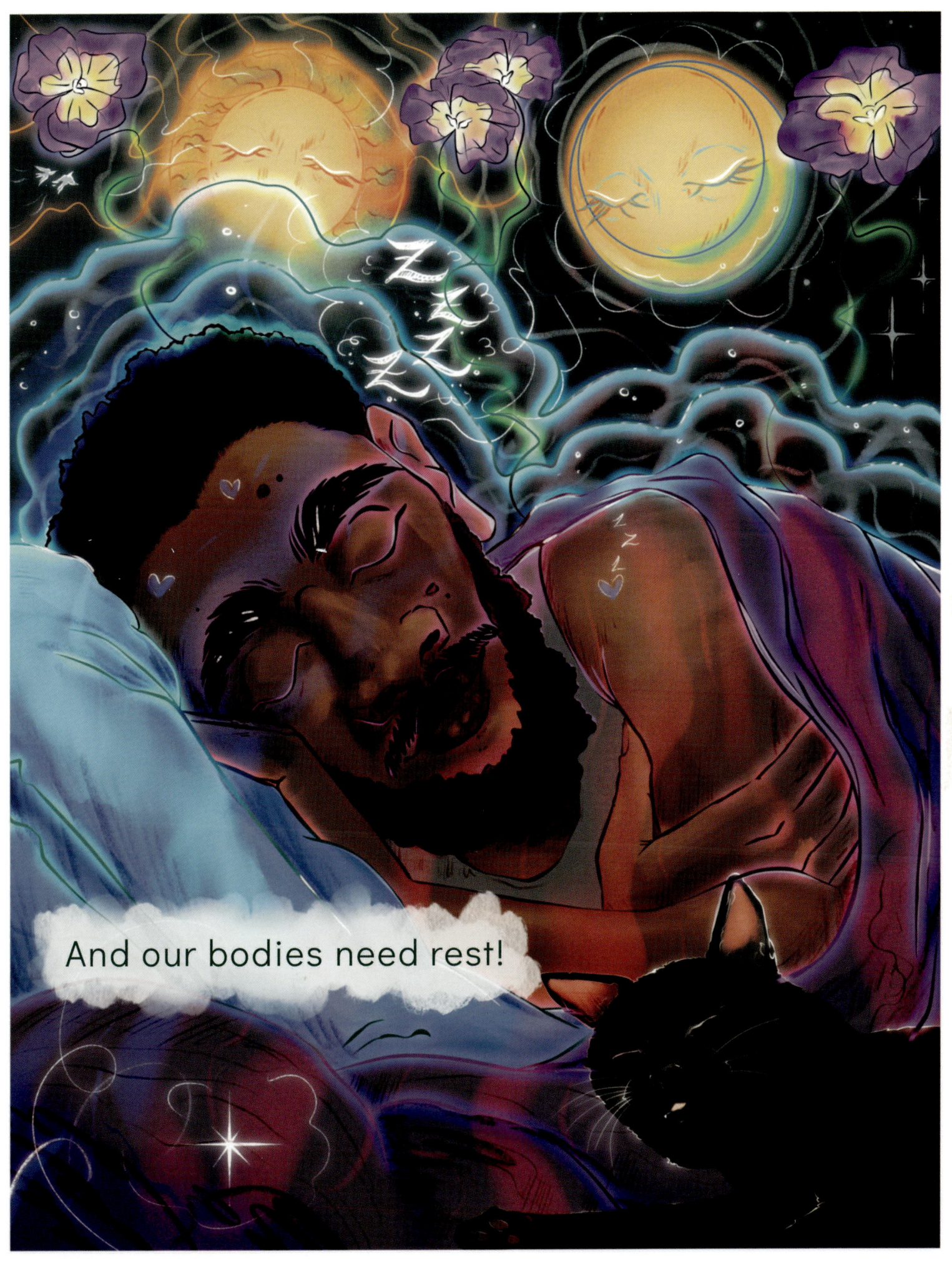

Sometimes space is best.

Some people are tall.

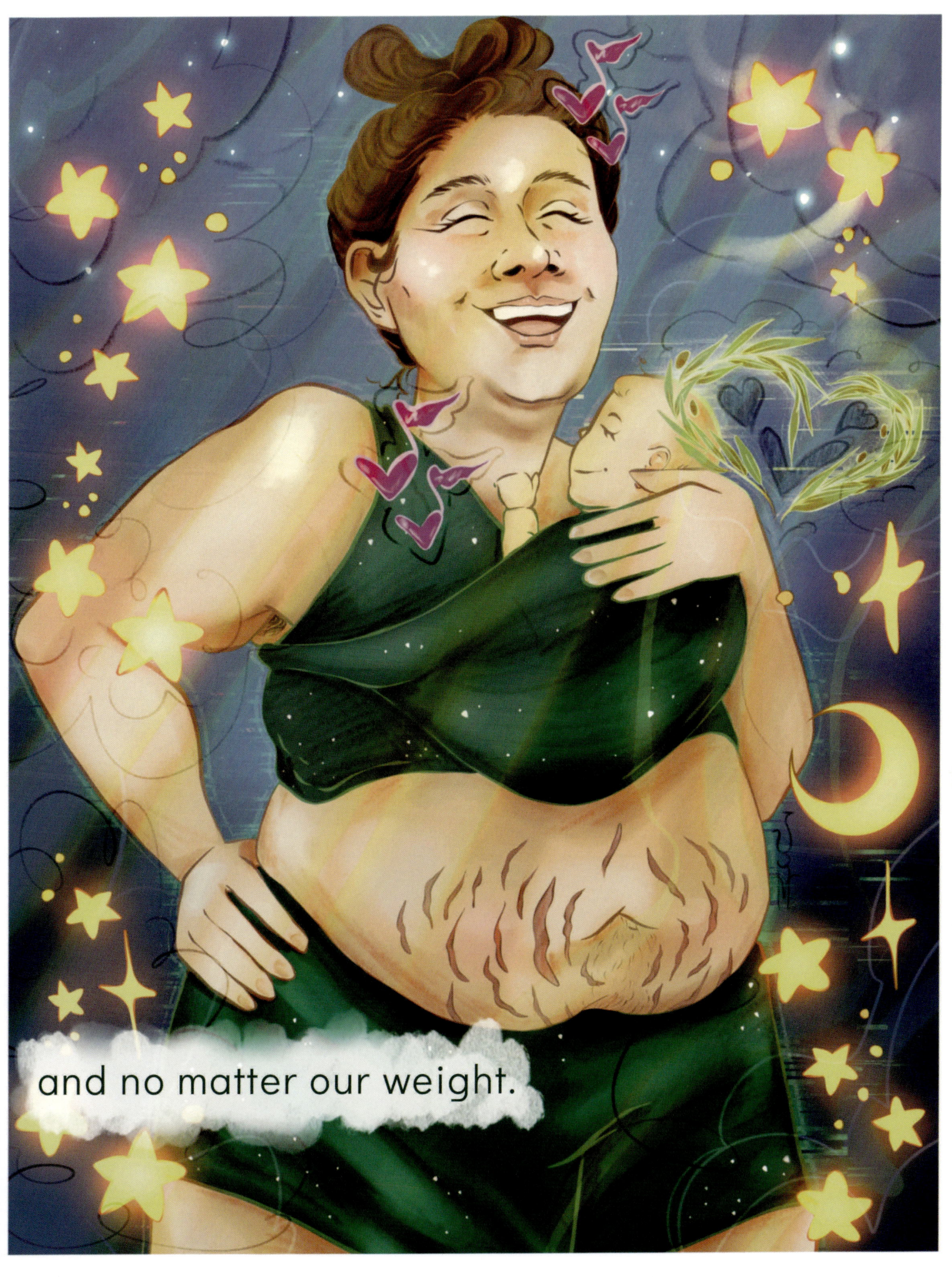

All bodies are important!

To my Olive:

Your body will carry you through this life and take you on every beautiful, messy, incredible journey. It will change in shape, size, and strength as you grow. Eat your favorite foods! Dance just because you feel like dancing! Climb mountains, take 3 hour naps, and tell yourself how wonderful you are! It is your home, and home is what you are to me. Never forget how special you are, my baby.

Want to know a secret?

I love you so much!

"Momom"

the illustrator of this book listens to a lot of music as part of their creative process. thank you to the following musicians whose albums have provided them with countless hours of creative energy for the duration of working on this book:

Solange, Phoenix, Vagabon, Djo, BAYLI, Gorillaz, Hovvdy, Abel Selaocoe, Hop Along, The Voidz, The Shins, Coconut Records, Vampire Weekend, CAKE, St. Vincent, Daft Punk, John Hennessey Baker, Albert Hammond Jr., Miike Snow, The Envy Corps, OK Go, Fleet Foxes, and The Strokes.

Use this page to draw your body!

Use this page to draw a body different than yours!